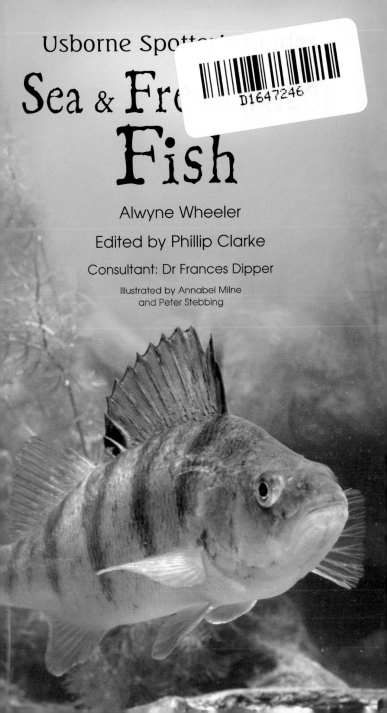

Usborne Spotter's Guide

Sea & Freshwater Fish

Alwyne Wheeler

Edited by Phillip Clarke

Consultant: Dr Frances Dipper

Illustrated by Annabel Milne
and Peter Stebbing

D1647246

Usborne Quicklinks

The Usborne Quicklinks Website is packed with thousands of links to all the best websites on the internet. The websites include information, video clips, sounds, games and animations that support and enhance the information in Usborne internet-linked books.

To visit the recommended websites for Spotter's Sea and Freshwater Fish, go to the Usborne Quicklinks Website at **www.usborne-quicklinks.com** and enter the keywords: **spotters fish**

Internet safety

When using the internet please follow the internet safety guidelines displayed on the Usborne Quicklinks Website. The recommended websites in Usborne Quicklinks are regularly reviewed and updated, but Usborne Publishing Ltd is not responsible for the content or availability of any website other than its own. We recommend that children are supervised while using the internet.

Usborne Publishing is not responsible and does not accept liability for the availability or content of any website other than its own, or for any exposure to harmful, offensive, or inaccurate material which may appear on the Web. Usborne Publishing will have no liability for any damage or loss caused by viruses that may be downloaded as a result of browsing the sites it recommends.

Contents

How to use this book

This book will help you to identify some of the fishes of Britain and Europe, both in the sea, and in freshwater habitats such as rivers or lakes. The fishes are grouped by the sea or freshwater zones in which they live. There's more information about this on pages 8–9.

Identification

All the different types, or species, of fish in this book have a picture and a description to help you identify them. The example below shows you how the descriptions work:

Fish features

Around the pictures are labels with more details about features that will help you to identify the fish.

Dark back, bronze sides

Mouth extends to pick up food

Useful words

If there are any words you don't understand, look at the list of useful words on page 59.

⬇ **Mediterranean Toothcarp** ——— Common name

In shallow pools at the sea's edge ——— Type of water in which it lives
and in marshy estuaries. Eats small
crustaceans and insect larvae. ——— What it eats
Mediterranean only. 5cm ——— Normal maximum length

Area in which it's found
(see map on page 5)

Circle to tick when you've spotted one

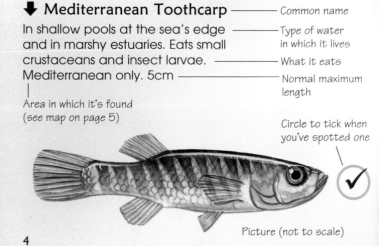

Picture (not to scale)

Map of Europe

This book covers the area shown in green on the map. Some fishes will not be seen, for example, in Britain, but may be spotted in other parts of Europe.

Greenland   Iceland

NORTH ATLANTIC OCEAN

Sweden

Norway

Finland

Northern Europe

Ireland

NORTH SEA

BALTIC SEA

Great Britain

Nether-lands

ENGLISH CHANNEL

Central Europe

Eastern Europe

Western Europe

The Alps

BLACK SEA

Southern Europe

Portugal Spain

NORTH ATLANTIC OCEAN

MEDITERRANEAN SEA

Fish names

A fish species may have lots of common names, but only ever one scientific name (in *italics*). These are included in the index at the back of the book, along with some other common names.

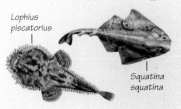

Lophius piscatorius

Squatina squatina

These fishes are both called Monkfish, but have unique scientific names.

Scorecard

On page 60 is a scorecard, giving you an idea of how common each species is, and how easy it is to spot. You can use it to keep score on a day out spotting. A common fish scores 5 points, and a very rare one is worth 25.

Species (name)	Score	Spotted
Meagre	20	
Mediterranean Toothcarp	20	10/08
Minnow	5	
Montagu's Blenny	15	Penzance

You can use the scorecard to record when or where you first saw each fish.

5

What are fish?

Fish are vertebrates, which means they are animals with backbones. Nearly all fishes have fins and scales, and breathe using gills. There are three main groups:
(1) Most fishes have bone skeletons, and so are classed as "bony fishes".
(2) Sharks and rays. These have skeletons made of flexible cartilage (gristle).

(3) Hagfish and lampreys. They also have cartilage skeletons but, unlike other fishes, have no jawbone.

Some water creatures, such as dolphins, look like fish but belong to a group of animals called mammals. These have lungs, not gills, so, unlike fish, they need to come up to the surface to breathe air.

Parts of a bony fish

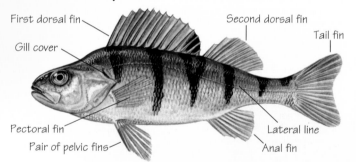

First dorsal fin

Gill cover

Second dorsal fin

Tail fin

Pectoral fin

Pair of pelvic fins

Lateral line

Anal fin

Breathing under water

Fish breathe using organs called gills that absorb oxygen from the water into their bloodstream. As fish swim, they gulp water into their mouths. It passes over the gills, and is pushed out again as the gill covers open.

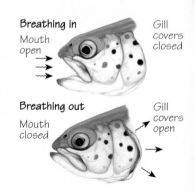

Breathing in
Mouth open

Gill covers closed

Breathing out
Mouth closed

Gill covers open

Shape and movement

Most fishes have streamlined bodies, and swim by swishing their tails from side to side. The fastest have torpedo-shaped bodies and crescent-shaped tails. Slow-swimming fishes, such as those that live on the bottom, rarely have streamlined bodies. They often don't use their tail-fin as much to swim, and may use other fins instead. Rays, for example, are bottom-living fish that swim using large, wing-like pectoral fins.

Dorsal fin

Anal fin

Ocean Sunfish have virtually no tail, and swim by moving their long dorsal and anal fins from side to side at the same time.

Tuna swim in the open ocean. Their bodies and tails are shaped for speed.

Anglerfish shuffle across the seafloor, using their large pectoral fins like legs.

Dorsal fin

Seahorses are unusual fish with upright bodies. They propel themselves slowly with a small dorsal fin.

Thornback Rays swim by flexing their fins with a wave-like motion.

Sea and freshwater zones

Bodies of water such as oceans, seas and rivers are divided into distinct zones. Different fishes are able to live in each of them.

The illustrations below show some examples of the types of fish that can be found living in each sea or freshwater zone.

Freshwater zones

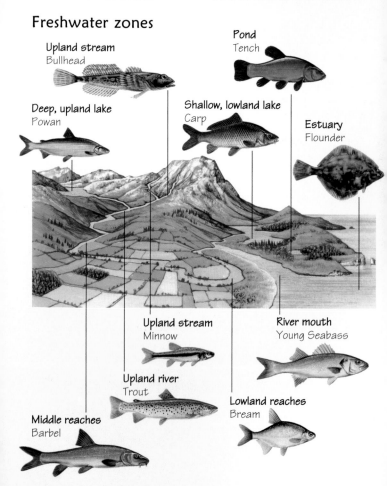

Pond
Tench

Upland stream
Bullhead

Deep, upland lake
Powan

Shallow, lowland lake
Carp

Estuary
Flounder

Upland stream
Minnow

River mouth
Young Seabass

Upland river
Trout

Lowland reaches
Bream

Middle reaches
Barbel

Few fishes can live in fast-flowing upland rivers. The calmer, food-rich "lowland reaches" hold the largest variety of freshwater fish. Many sea fishes live near the sunlit surface, feeding in large groups, called schools, on the plankton that thrives there. Midwater fishes feed mainly on crustaceans and other fishes. Bottom-living fishes often eat seabed creatures, such as worms.

Ocean zones

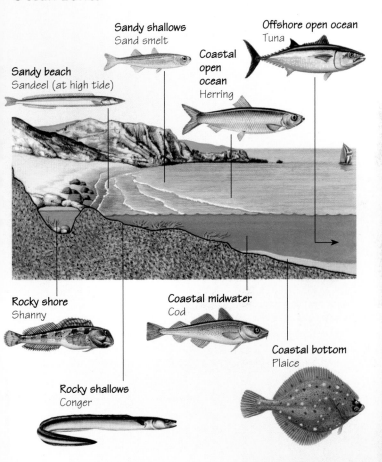

Sandy shallows
Sand smelt

Offshore open ocean
Tuna

Coastal open ocean
Herring

Sandy beach
Sandeel (at high tide)

Rocky shore
Shanny

Coastal midwater
Cod

Coastal bottom
Plaice

Rocky shallows
Conger

Spotting fish

Fish like to hide from view, so spotting them can be hard. Here are a few tips.

Where to look

Rivers, streams and canals
Riverbanks or low bridges are good vantage points. In fast streams, look for fish sheltering by small boulders.

Lakes and ponds
Find a jetty or low bank, and look out for water plants where fish may hide.

Seaside
A sheltered, weedy beach is the best place to spot lots of seashore fish.

Aquariums
Some rare fishes, such as sturgeon, may only be seen in aquariums.

What to take

- Notebook and pencils for drawing and note-taking
- Shrimp net and jam jars for collecting little fishes
- Pieces of bread or cheese to put in the jars as bait
- Tape measure or clear, plastic ruler to measure fish
- A clear, plastic box you can lower into ponds or rockpools, to use as an underwater viewer
- Polarized sunglasses to reduce glare, making fish easier to see under water
- Sturdy footwear and an old towel, to walk and kneel on barnacle-encrusted rocks
- This book!

Sensitive to weather, fish hide from bright sun and storms, emerging as conditions change.

When to go

There's always lots to see in rivers and seas, but some times of the day and year are better for spotting than others. At the seaside, many fishes swim in the shallows an hour before low tide. Spring is a good time to see fish in rockpools; summer is ideal for snorkelling.

Freshwater fishes are most active in the early morning and evening. In spring, seek out egg-guarding fishes such as Bullheads. Look for Minnows in shallow streams in summer. In autumn, look out for Salmon returning from the sea to breed.

Top tips

- Be patient, and keep still: sudden motion scares fish.
- Don't wear bright colours or let your shadow fall across the water.
- Always return any fishes to where you found them.

Safety first

- Always tell someone where you're going.
- Never go alone.
- Watch out for severe weather warnings.

Rivers, lakes and ponds
- Don't wade out into rivers: undercurrents can be dangerous.
- Beware of balancing on logs or stepping stones: they may tip over.

Seaside
- Check tide times, to avoid being stranded.
- Only go snorkelling* if you're a strong swimmer. Tie a whistle to your snorkel, to call for help if you need it.

* *Sign up for a session in a swimming pool, to learn techniques before you go.*

Camouflage

Whether they're hunting or being hunted, fishes have a range of ways to avoid being seen. Camouflage is one of the most effective:

Concealment is a type of camouflage in which a fish's colour matches its background. Many sea fishes are concealed by being dark on top and pale below. This is called **countershading**.

Mackerel

A Mackerel, seen from above, blends in with the gloomy depths.

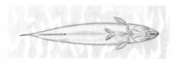

From below, its white belly is hard to see against the sunny surface.

Disguise is camouflage where a fish naturally looks like part of the scenery.

This Worm Pipefish looks like a piece of seaweed.

Disruption camouflage works by breaking up a fish's outline so that it's hard to make out.

A Pike's tigerish stripes help it to lurk undetected in the weeds.

Mimicry is camouflage in which one animal resembles another that its predators would normally avoid.

This Butterfish's spots look enough like eyes to confuse a predator.

Breeding behaviour

At breeding time, some fishes perform elaborate routines to attract a mate. For instance, in early summer, male Three-spined Sticklebacks build nests, then dance to attract the females to lay their eggs inside them.

Male

The male Three-spined Stickleback builds a nest out of water plants.

Once the female Stickleback has laid her eggs, she leaves the nest.

The male protects the eggs, and guards the fry (young) when they've hatched.

Some fishes travel a long way to lay their eggs. For example, European Eels breed in a weedy area of the Atlantic called the Sargasso Sea. Eel larvae slowly drift to Europe, where they go through a series of changes.

(2) Flat, see-through eel larvae (**Leptocephali**) take a year or more to reach Europe.

(1) Eggs

(3) Young eels called **Elvers** move into river estuaries, and then swim up rivers.

(5) **Silver Eels** return to their birthplace in the sea to breed, lay their eggs, and die.

(4) **Yellow Eels** continue up streams, where they may live for 5–30 years.

13

Mouths and feeding

The shape and position of a fish's mouth can tell you what sort of food it eats, and whether it feeds on the surface or at the bottom. Surface feeders have upward-facing mouths; those of bottom feeders face downwards, or are low-set. Fishes that eat other fish have wide mouths and sharp teeth.

Freshwater

Bleak – Feeds near the surface on plankton and insects. Upward-facing mouth.

Brown Trout – Feeds at all levels, on crustaceans, fishes and insects. Large, toothed jaws for catching big prey.

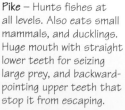

Nase – Feeds on green algae, scraping it off rocks with its rough-lipped, slit-like mouth.

Pike – Hunts fishes at all levels. Also eats small mammals, and ducklings. Huge mouth with straight lower teeth for seizing large prey, and backward-pointing upper teeth that stop it from escaping.

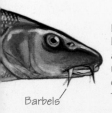

Barbel – Feeds at the bottom on insects, larvae and worms. Fleshy, low-set mouth. It is named because of its barbels, which it uses to feel for prey in the gravel.

Barbels

Hunting for food in the ocean is very competitive, and some fishes have specialized features to help them. Swordfish, for example, use their long bills to knock out small fish before eating them.

Anglerfish attract little fish with a dangling lure attached to their head. Electric Rays stun their prey with an electric shock. Basking Sharks have huge gills with long, comb-like "rakers" that trap plankton.

Sea

Mackerel

Swordfish

Hake

Conger

Sole

Mackerel – Feeds mostly near the surface, on small fishes and crustaceans. Large mouth.

Swordfish – Feeds on fishes near the surface. Large mouth.

Hake – Feeds in midwater at night on fishes and squid. Big, wide mouth with many sharp teeth to hold slippery prey.

Conger – In holes and under rocks. A constant hunter of large fish, crabs and octopuses. Huge mouth and rows of sharp, cutting teeth.

Sole – Lives on the seabed, feeding on crustaceans and worms. Its small, semi-circular mouth extends underneath its body.

15

Upland streams and lakes

In upland streams, the water is usually clear, cold and fast-flowing. The fishes shelter behind or under rocks. In upland lakes, many of the fishes spend the winter in deep water.

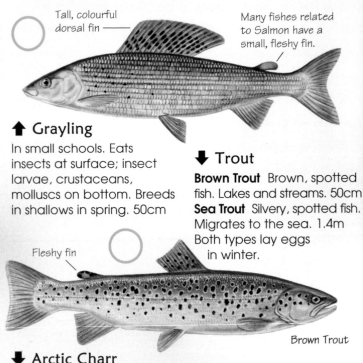

Tall, colourful dorsal fin ——

Many fishes related to Salmon have a small, fleshy fin.

⬆ Grayling

In small schools. Eats insects at surface; insect larvae, crustaceans, molluscs on bottom. Breeds in shallows in spring. 50cm

⬇ Trout

Brown Trout Brown, spotted fish. Lakes and streams. 50cm
Sea Trout Silvery, spotted fish. Migrates to the sea. 1.4m
Both types lay eggs in winter.

Fleshy fin

Brown Trout

⬇ Arctic Charr

Mainly in lakes, but in northern countries lives in rivers and sea. Eats small crustaceans, insects, fishes. May live for 25 years. In rivers, 1m. In mountain lakes, 25cm

Lake Charr; sea-going Charr more silvery

➡ Vendace

Found in mountain lakes in Britain and the Alps, and in the Baltic Sea. Eats mainly fish and crustaceans. 25cm

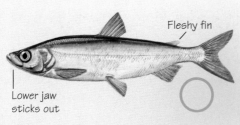

Fleshy fin

Lower jaw sticks out

⬅ Powan

A rare fish found only in a few Scottish lochs and reservoirs. Feeds on small crustaceans, and insects. 20cm

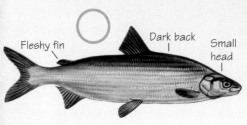

Fleshy fin

Dark back

Small head

➡ Minnow

Large schools near surface often in shallow streams. Eats insects, their larvae, and crustaceans. 8cm

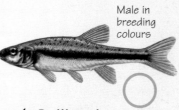

Male in breeding colours

⬅ Bullhead

Hides under rocks and in dense plant growth by day. Active at dusk and dawn. Lays eggs in a gap under a large stone. 10cm

Wide head and mouth

Large pectoral fins

⬇ Streber

Slender, bottom-living, mainly solitary fish. Found in eastern Europe. Lives in fast-flowing streams. Eats insect larvae and crustaceans, mainly at night. 15cm

Long, narrow tail

Dark bars

Middle reaches

In the middle reaches, the water current is moderate
with fast-flowing stretches, and also slower deep pools.
The water is fairly clear and there are lots of water plants.

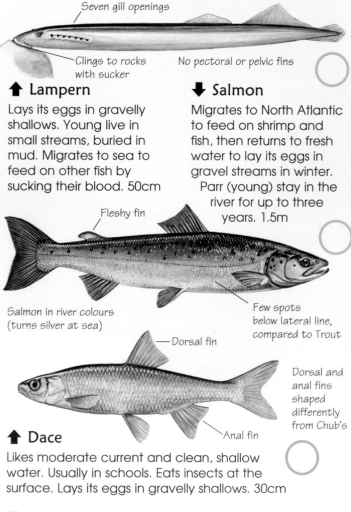

Seven gill openings

Clings to rocks
with sucker

No pectoral or pelvic fins

⬆ Lampern

Lays its eggs in gravelly
shallows. Young live in
small streams, buried in
mud. Migrates to sea to
feed on other fish by
sucking their blood. 50cm

⬇ Salmon

Migrates to North Atlantic
to feed on shrimp and
fish, then returns to fresh
water to lay its eggs in
gravel streams in winter.
Parr (young) stay in the
river for up to three
years. 1.5m

Fleshy fin

Salmon in river colours
(turns silver at sea)

Few spots
below lateral line,
compared to Trout

Dorsal fin

Dorsal and
anal fins
shaped
differently
from Chub's

⬆ Dace

Anal fin

Likes moderate current and clean, shallow
water. Usually in schools. Eats insects at the
surface. Lays its eggs in gravelly shallows. 30cm

⬆ Barbel

Lives at bottom in moderate currents. Active at dawn and dusk. Seeks food in gravel beds with its four barbels (feelers). 90cm

⬇ Nase

Schools in fast currents among rocks or below weirs and waterfalls. Eats green algae off rocks. Central Europe. 50cm

Fleshy "nose"

Tail colour may vary from black to red

Dorsal and tail fins are dark grey

⬇ Chub

Swims in schools when young, but large fish live alone in deep pools under trees and river banks. Eats fish, insects and crayfish. 50cm

Thick, white lips

➡ Bleak

Lives in schools at the water's surface. Eats water fleas, other crustaceans, and insects. 15cm

Upward-facing mouth

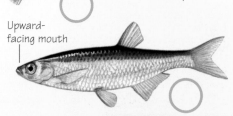

19

Middle reaches

➡ Stone Loach

Hides under stones or in weed-beds by day. Hunts for insect larvae, crustaceans and worms on the bottom at night. 10cm

Front of body rounded

Six barbels

Breeding male

⬅ Three-spined Stickleback

In rivers, lakes and ponds (and sea) in northern Europe. Eats small crustaceans. Nests near the bottom. Breeding male has red belly (see also page 13). 5cm

⬆ Asp

Prefers mild currents but will live in lakes. Young form schools; adults mainly solitary and eat fish. Not in Spain. Rare in northern Europe. 60cm

Lower fins red

⬇ Perch

Usually in large schools. Young lurk under bridges and jetties; bigger ones live in deeper water. All eat smaller fishes and insect larvae. 51cm

Spines jut out of dorsal fin

Dark stripes on sides

Lower fins orangey-red

Lowland lakes and ponds

These include reservoirs, gravel-workings and farm ponds. The water varies from clear and well-oxygenated to murky and stagnant. Most lowland waters are full of animal and plant life, so the fish that live here grow large quickly.

➡ **Ninespine Stickleback**

In dense weed-beds, or even ditches. Male makes a nest just off the bottom. He guards the eggs. 7cm

7–12 spines on back

Male in dark breeding colours

Dorsal fin curves outwards

Humped back

No barbels

⬇ **Common Carp**

Prefers warm, weedy lakes. Feeds mainly on bottom-living worms and molluscs. "Mirror" variety has patches of big, shiny scales; "Leather" Carp has no scales. 61cm

⬆ **Crucian Carp**

Lives in marshy pools and lakes, in thick weed. In May–June it lays golden eggs on the leaves of water plants. 51cm

Long dorsal fin with saw-like edge

Two pairs of barbels

Fully scaled Common variety

21

Lowland lakes and ponds

⬇ Tench

Lives in thick weed-beds. Burrows in mud in winter. Eats insect larvae, snails, crustaceans, sometimes plants. 50cm

Slimy skin with small scales

Little red eyes

Thick tail

Barbels

⬇ Mudminnow

Lives in swamps and overgrown ponds. Feeds mainly on bottom-living insect larvae. Lays its eggs in spring. Eastern Europe only. Now rare. 13cm

Stripe may be paler

⬇ Weatherfish

A type of loach that lives in stagnant ponds. If the oxygen gets too low, it swallows air at the surface. Active at night but may appear by day in thundery weather. Northern and eastern Europe only. 25cm

Ten barbels

⬇ Rainbow Trout

North American fish introduced into Europe. Young eat insects, their larvae, and crustaceans. Adults eat other fish. 1m

Pinkish-red stripe

Fleshy fin

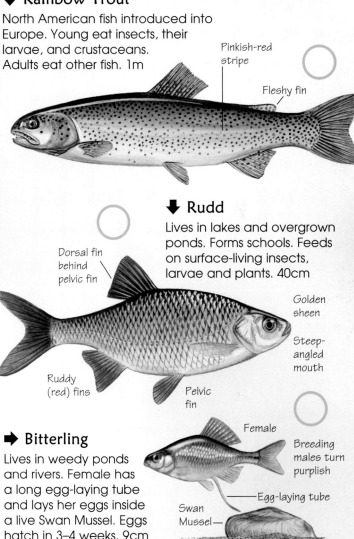

⬇ Rudd

Lives in lakes and overgrown ponds. Forms schools. Feeds on surface-living insects, larvae and plants. 40cm

Dorsal fin behind pelvic fin

Golden sheen

Steep-angled mouth

Ruddy (red) fins

Pelvic fin

Female

➡ Bitterling

Lives in weedy ponds and rivers. Female has a long egg-laying tube and lays her eggs inside a live Swan Mussel. Eggs hatch in 3–4 weeks. 9cm

Breeding males turn purplish

Egg-laying tube

Swan Mussel

Lowland reaches

A river's lowland reaches wind lazily through gently sloping land. Fishes there like the cloudy water, mild current and muddy bottom. Thick weed-beds at the sides provide food, shelter and places to lay eggs.

➡ Goldfish

A type of Carp, first kept as a pet in China. Now widespread in Europe where pet fish have escaped. In dense weed, where it lays eggs in June–July. 30cm

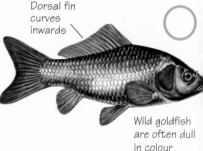

Dorsal fin curves inwards

Wild goldfish are often dull in colour

⬇ Pike

Hides among water plants waiting to attack prey. Eats all but biggest fishes, and sometimes ducklings and water mammals. Lives up to 20 years. Female 1.3m Male 70cm

⬇ Gudgeon

Small schools in rivers and canals, close to bottom on mud and gravel. Eats crustaceans, snails and insect larvae. 15cm

Gudgeon squeak to each other

Long barbels

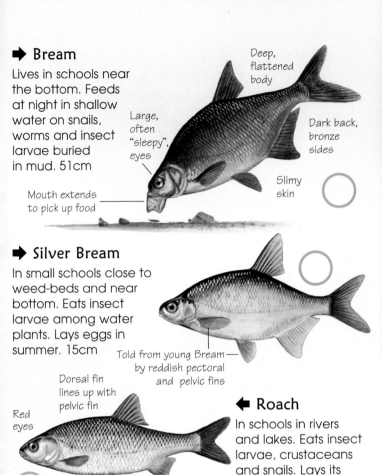

➡ Bream

Lives in schools near the bottom. Feeds at night in shallow water on snails, worms and insect larvae buried in mud. 51cm

Deep, flattened body

Large, often "sleepy", eyes

Dark back, bronze sides

Slimy skin

Mouth extends to pick up food

➡ Silver Bream

In small schools close to weed-beds and near bottom. Eats insect larvae among water plants. Lays eggs in summer. 15cm

Told from young Bream by reddish pectoral and pelvic fins

Dorsal fin lines up with pelvic fin

Red eyes

Pelvic fin

⬅ Roach

In schools in rivers and lakes. Eats insect larvae, crustaceans and snails. Lays its eggs in April–June on water plants. 50cm

⬇ Spined Loach

Lives in soft mud and green algae. Comes out at night to feed on tiny crustaceans. Spine under each eye. 11.5cm

Sides of body flattened

Lowland reaches

No scales

Six barbels

⬆ Wels Catfish

The only native European catfish. In deep, still water, and lakes. Hunts mostly at night. Eats mainly fish, but also frogs, ducks and voles. Huge, up to 3m

⬇ Burbot

Only freshwater Cod-like fish. Lives under tree roots and in holes in banks. Active mainly at night. Extinct in Britain. 51cm

Raised nostrils

Fins joined together

⬅ Ruffe

Forms small schools close to the bottom. Feeds on bloodworms (midge larvae) and crustaceans. Lives for up to five years. 18cm

⬇ Zander

Pike-like relative of Perch, also called Pike-perch. From central Europe but now found throughout northern Europe. Lives in cloudy water. Schools of Zander hunt smaller fishes, mainly at dawn and dusk. 70cm

River mouths and estuaries

The waters here are fresh upstream, salty at the river mouth, usually with a muddy bottom, mud banks and few plants.

Seven gill openings

↑ Sea Lamprey

Sucks the blood of bigger fishes. Adults migrate into fresh water to lay eggs, then die. Larvae spend several years buried in river mud. 91cm

↓ Sturgeon

Europe's biggest fish, other than sharks. Breeds in large rivers over a gravel bottom. Migrates to sea to feed on bottom-living fishes, crustaceans, molluscs and worms. Endangered. 3.5m

Bony plates

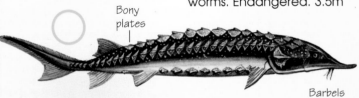

Barbels

Adult is called a Yellow Eel

← European Eel

Long, snaky body. Breeds in Atlantic. Changes appearance as it grows and swims inland up rivers and streams. (See page 13 for more details.) Endangered. 1m

↓ Twaite Shad

Large relative of Herring. Lives at sea but migrates up rivers to lay eggs in gravelly shallows. Eats crustaceans and small fishes. 55cm

Dark spots

27

River mouths and estuaries

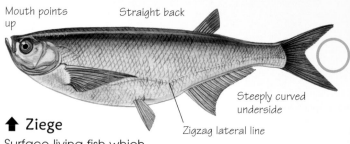

Mouth points up

Straight back

Steeply curved underside

Zigzag lateral line

⬆ Ziege

Surface-living fish which migrates in schools up rivers from the sea. Feeds mainly on fishes. Found in Baltic and Black Sea countries. Also known as Sabrefish. 51cm

⬇ Mediterranean Toothcarp

In shallow coastal pools and marshy estuaries. Eats small crustaceans and insect larvae. Mediterranean only. 6cm

⬇ Meagre

Uncommon in northern European seas, but elsewhere young are common in estuaries. Eats small fishes. Makes a loud drumming sound at breeding time. 2m

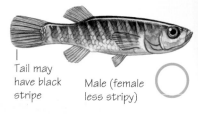

Tail may have black stripe

Male (female less stripy)

Fins greyer on smaller fish

Long second dorsal fin

Mouth orange inside

Rounded tail

⬆ Seabass

Strong-swimming
fish. Common in shallow
coastal waters and river
mouths. Eats Sandeels,
Sprats and other fishes;
squid and crabs. Rare
north of Britain. 1m

⬇ Thinlip Grey Mullet

Swims into river mouths in
schools from the sea. Eats
algae, and tiny creatures
in the mud. Rare north of
English Channel. 60cm

Mullet feeding on algae

High pectoral fins

Small
mouth

⬇ Flounder

Only European flatfish that
migrates into rivers and lives
in fresh water. Eats shrimp
and other crustaceans. Eyes
usually on right side of face.
River 30cm. Sea 50cm

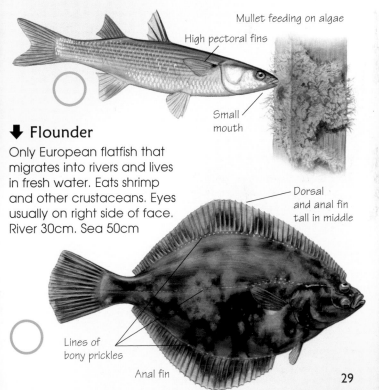

Dorsal
and anal fin
tall in middle

Lines of
bony prickles

Anal fin

29

Sandy beaches and shallows

Many fishes burrow into the sand in shallow water, coming out to look for food at night. These areas have no seaweed to hide in, so many fish often live in schools for protection.

↓ Fivebeard Rockling

Common in shallow water and on rocky shores. Young silvery with metallic blue-green backs, live at the sea surface. Not in Mediterranean. 25cm

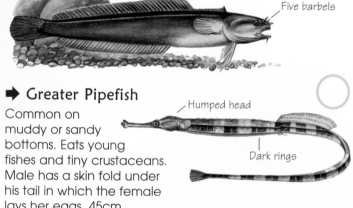

Five barbels

→ Greater Pipefish

Common on muddy or sandy bottoms. Eats young fishes and tiny crustaceans. Male has a skin fold under his tail in which the female lays her eggs. 45cm

Humped head

Dark rings

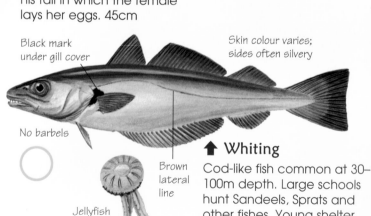

Black mark under gill cover

Skin colour varies; sides often silvery

No barbels

Brown lateral line

Jellyfish

↑ Whiting

Cod-like fish common at 30–100m depth. Large schools hunt Sandeels, Sprats and other fishes. Young shelter under jellyfishes. 40cm

Colour varies

Dip in fin

Fin continues around body

⬆ Eelpout

Common fish on sandy and rocky shores in pools, under stones and seaweed. Doesn't lay eggs, but gives birth to live young about 4cm long. North Atlantic only. 19cm

Bright silver stripe

⬇ Thicklip Grey Mullet

In coastal waters in large schools, migrating north in summer. Eats fine algae on rocks, and hoovers up seabed mud, filtering out tiny animals and shooting the waste out of its gills. 75cm

⬆ Sand Smelt

Usually in huge schools. Breeds in shore pools in summer. Eggs have long threads which get tangled with seaweeds. 9cm

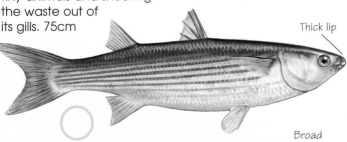

Thick lip

➡ Hooknose

Lives in shallow water 2–40m deep. Often caught in shrimp nets. Feeds on small crustaceans, worms and molluscs. 20cm

Dark bands

Broad head

Hook

Many barbels

31

Sandy beaches and shallows

➡ Lesser Weever

Lies buried in sand in shallow water, with its venomous spines sticking up. Feeds mostly on small shrimp and other crustaceans. **Do not touch**. 14cm

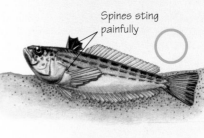

Spines sting painfully

Hump in lateral line

➡ Dab

Very common in shallow water on sandy or muddy bottoms. Often seen by paddlers. Eats small crustaceans. Not in Mediterranean. 25cm

⬇ Small Sandeel

In huge schools close to the bottom. Burrows head-first in the sand. Eaten by other fishes, and birds such as Terns and Puffins. Rare in Mediterranean. 20cm

Lower jaw juts forward—

⬇ Sand Goby

Lives on sandy shores to 10m deep. Eats small crustaceans and is often eaten by birds and fishes. Lays its eggs in an old mollusc shell. 9cm

Blue-black spot

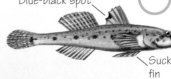

Sucker fin

Rocky shores and shallows

These areas are rich in animal and plant life. Fishes live in pools, under stones or among seaweed. Many spend most of their lives on the same shore.

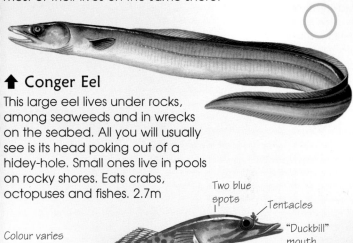

⬆ Conger Eel

This large eel lives under rocks, among seaweeds and in wrecks on the seabed. All you will usually see is its head poking out of a hidey-hole. Small ones live in pools on rocky shores. Eats crabs, octopuses and fishes. 2.7m

Colour varies from reddish to green

Two blue spots

Tentacles

"Duckbill" mouth

Sucker fin

Spots

⬆ Shore Clingfish

Also called Cornish Sucker. Lives under rocks and boulders. Clings with its strong sucker. Golden eggs can be found in summer, guarded by the parents. 6.5cm

➡ Worm Pipefish

Lives among brown seaweeds in rockpools and is very hard to see. Males have a shallow groove on the belly in which the female lays eggs. Not in the Mediterranean. 15cm

Stubby snout

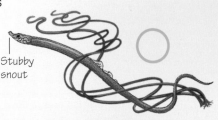

Rocky shores and shallows

Strongly curved lateral line

Lower jaw sticks out

⬆ Pollack
Cod-like fish. Adults school in midwater, close to rocks. Eats fishes, especially Sandeels and Herrings. Not in eastern Mediterranean. 1.3m

⬇ Shore Rockling
Most common on rocky shores in pools and under seaweed. Its three barbels help it to locate shrimp, small crabs and worms, which it eats. 35cm

Three barbels

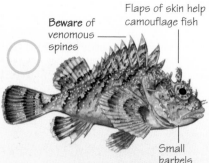

Beware of venomous spines

Flaps of skin help camouflage fish

Small barbels

⬅ Scorpionfish
Lies motionless among rocks and under seaweeds in shallow water. Hunts for crustaceans and fish at night. Rare in North Atlantic. 25cm

← Cardinalfish

In small groups in caves or crevices in rocky outcrops. Hunts actively at night. Male holds the eggs in his mouth until they hatch. Mediterranean. 15cm

→ Sea Scorpion

Common in rockpools and among seaweeds. Related to Bullhead (see page 17). Eats shrimp, small crabs and fishes. 17cm

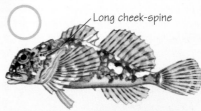

Long cheek-spine

Changes colour to camouflage itself

Some have dark vertical stripes

↑ Comber

Lives over seagrass beds and around rocky outcrops. Eats small fishes and crustaceans. Rare in north Atlantic. 30cm

↓ Sea Stickleback

Lives entirely in the sea among seaweeds and eel-grass. Male builds a cup-sized nest in the seaweed. Not found in Mediterranean. 15cm

Brown stripe through eye

14–16 spines

Rocky shores and shallows

➡ Short-snouted Seahorse

Lives among seaweeds and other plants. Clings to them with its tail. The female lays her eggs in the male's belly pouch. Mates for life. Uncommon. 15cm

Changes colour to hide among weeds

Egg pouch

⬇ Lumpsucker

Uses its strong sucker to cling to rocks when guarding its eggs in spring. These are sold as "lumpfish roe". North Atlantic. 50cm

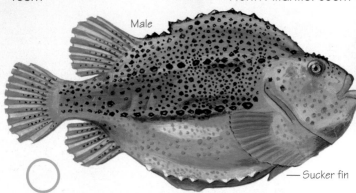

Male

Sucker fin

➡ Grey Triggerfish

Spines can be locked in an upright position, so that the fish cannot be dragged out of rock crevices

Adults live near rocks, wrecks, marinas and piers. Young live out at sea, among drifting weed. Eats molluscs, crustaceans. Mediterranean, Atlantic. 35cm

Colour varies from greenish-grey to brown

➡ Damselfish

Very common in Mediterranean. Forms large schools close to rocks or seagrass meadows. Feeds on plankton. Lays its eggs on flat patches of rock. Male guards the eggs. 15cm

Young Damselfish are bright blue

Broad, black bands

⬅ Two-banded Bream

Common in small groups close to seaweed-strewn rocks. Eats crustaceans and worms. Lays eggs in winter. Mediterranean, Black Sea, North Atlantic from Portugal to Northern France. 25cm

⬇ Saddled Bream

In small schools close to rocks and seagrass beds, often 2–3m below the surface. Eats small, bottom-living creatures and seaweeds. Southern Europe. 30cm

Black "saddle" ringed with white

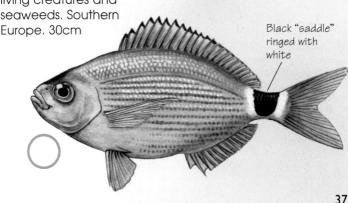

Rocky shores and shallows

➡ Parrotfish

Small groups swim around rocks and scrape algae off them with their strong teeth. Mediterranean, Atlantic south of Spain. 50cm

Broad teeth make mouth look like a parrot's beak

Black spot on tail

⬅ Goldsinny Wrasse

Lives close to weedy rocks and in eelgrass beds. Eats small crustaceans and molluscs and picks parasites off the bodies of larger fishes. 15cm

➡ Ocellated Wrasse

In Mediterranean at moderate depths near rocks and seagrass. Builds seaweed nest. Young eat parasites off other fishes. 13cm

Dark smudge

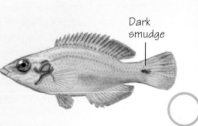

⬅ Five-spotted Wrasse

In shallow water among rocks and eelgrass. Male makes large seaweed nest for female's eggs. He guards the eggs. Mediterranean. 15cm

Up to five blackish marks on dorsal fin

Mottled pattern; colour varies

Young are bright, lime green

⬆ Ballan Wrasse

Large wrasse. Common except in Mediterranean. Lives in rocky places. Feeds mainly on shellfish such as mussels. 60cm

⬇ Cuckoo Wrasse

Uncommon. Lives by rocks. A white patch appears on the males' heads at breeding time. Some females turn into males. 35cm

Breeding male

Females pink-orange with black and white marks by their tails

➡ Rainbow Wrasse

Common in Mediterranean, near rocks and in seagrass beds. Lives in small schools led by the biggest male. Females turn into males with age. 25cm

Adult male; female plainer

⬅ Ornate Wrasse

Common in Mediterranean among weedy rocks at about 20m. Females often change into males as they grow older. 20cm

Male; females have blue stripes on body

39

Rocky shores and shallows

This Blenny has scales and three dorsal fins

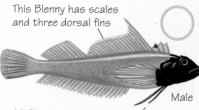

Male

All Blennies on this page have long, thin pelvic fins

← Black-faced Blenny

Found on rocky shores in shallow water. Male has a territory about 1m wide which he defends. Female is mottled brown. Mainly in Mediterranean. 8cm

→ Montagu's Blenny

In rockpools almost bare of seaweeds. Eats barnacles that live on the rocks, biting off their feathery limbs as they extend from their shells. 8.5cm

Triangular tentacle on head

This and the Blennies below have single dorsal fins, and no scales

No tentacles

↑ Shanny

Very common type of Blenny in pools and among seaweeds on sandy and rocky shores. Eats small crustaceans. 16cm

↓ Peacock Blenny

In very shallow water on mud and sand near rocks. Lays eggs under empty shells or in hollows in rocks. Mediterranean. 10cm

Dark spot

Blennies can change skin colour

In breeding males, first
dorsal fin has orange tip

Sucker fin —

⬆ Rock Goby

On rocky shores in
pools and under
stones. Lays eggs in
crevices. 12cm

Male has dark spot
behind pectoral fin

Dark spot

Sucker fin

⬇ Butterfish

In shallow water and
under stones on shore.
Female wraps herself
around her eggs. Not in
Mediterranean. 20cm

⬆ Two-spotted Goby

In small schools close to rocks
and seaweeds, and in deep
rockpools. Male guards the
eggs in early summer, often in
a hollow seaweed "root". 6cm

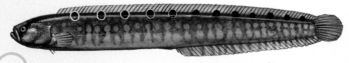

Changes colour to
match its surroundings

Very slippery skin
(hence its name)

➡ Eckström's Topknot

V-shaped marking

Lives on rocky bottoms
in depths of 9-55m,
and may cling to
the underside of
rocks. Rarely
caught.
12cm

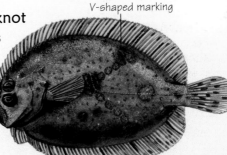

Coastal bottom-living fishes

Many of these fishes burrow in the sandy seabed, or change their colouring to match it. Others take shelter in rocky areas and shipwrecks.

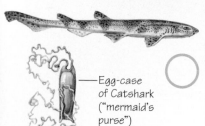

Egg-case of Catshark ("mermaid's purse")

← Small-spotted Catshark

Small, common shark. Lays eggs in cases called mermaid's purses, with long tendrils that curl around seaweeds. Eats crabs, shrimp and fishes. 1m

Gill openings

↑ Sand Tiger

Mainly in deep water but comes into sandy shallows. Eats fish and squid, but will attack any larger animal. **Dangerous** to bathers and paddlers. Mediterranean and further south. 3m

→ Angelshark

Bottom-living shark found in sand or mud in depths of 5–90m. Eats flatfishes and rays. Gives birth to up to 20 young at a time. Endangered (extinct in North Sea). 1.8m

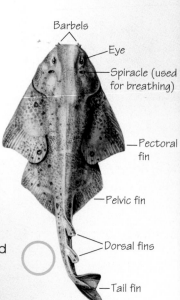

Barbels

Eye

Spiracle (used for breathing)

Pectoral fin

Pelvic fin

Dorsal fins

Tail fin

➡ Electric Ray

In depths of 10–150m.
Uses electric organs in
each "wing" to stun
fish with a powerful
electric shock. **Do
not touch**. 1.8m

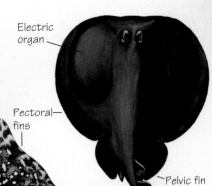

Electric
organ

Pectoral—
fins

Pelvic fin

The colour
of these two
rays varies

Pectoral
fin

Pelvic fin

No dorsal fins

⬅ Thornback Ray

Common at depths of 10–
60m on sand or mud. Eats
crustaceans, fishes. Lays
eggs in oblong egg-case
("mermaid's purse"). 85cm

⬅ Stingray

At depths of 3–70m on
sand or mud. Visits northern
seas in summer. **Beware** of
dangerous tail spine. 1.4m

Stinging
spine

➡ Moray Eel

In rock crevices and
under boulders. Hunts
for fishes at night. **Bites
savagely** if handled.
Southern Europe and
Mediterranean. 1.3m

Colour varies

Coastal bottom-living fishes

➡ Tub Gurnard

Common on muddy and sandy bottoms. Feels for food with its finger-like rays. Grunts when frightened. 75cm

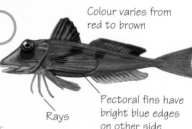

Colour varies from red to brown

Pectoral fins have bright blue edges on other side

Rays

⬅ Flying gurnard

Lives close to muddy or sandy bottoms. Spreads its brightly coloured fins to scare off predators. Mediterranean and north to English Channel. 50cm

Huge, fan-like pectoral fins

(Seen from above)

➡ Anglerfish

Lies buried in sandy, shelly or muddy bottoms. Has a worm-like lure on its head to attract small fishes towards its mouth. Sold as "Monkfish". 2m

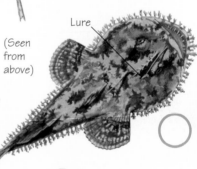

Lure

⬇ Stargazer

Mostly Mediterranean. Lies buried in sand, wiggling its tongue like a worm to lure small fishes. Detects them with weak electric currents. 25cm

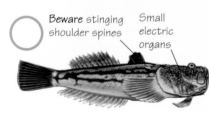

Beware stinging shoulder spines

Small electric organs

➡ Red Bandfish

Burrows in stiff mud at depths of 15–400m. Pops out of its hole to snap up small, passing crustaceans. 50cm

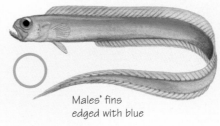

Males' fins edged with blue

Spiracle (used for breathing when fish is hiding in the seabed)

⬆ Sawfish

Related to rays. Uses its long, toothed snout to stir up hidden molluscs, crustaceans and fishes in sand and mud. Southern Europe. Near-extinct (hunted for snout and fins). 4.5m

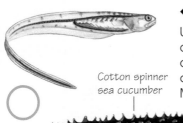

⬅ Pearlfish

Usually lives inside a sea cucumber. Eats the internal organs of its host. Also pops out to catch small animals. Mediterranean. 20cm

Cotton spinner sea cucumber

➡ Red Mullet

In small schools close to the bottom. Uses its long barbels to search for food. Young fish are silvery-blue and live at the surface of the sea. 35cm

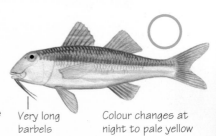

Very long barbels

Colour changes at night to pale yellow

Coastal bottom-living fishes

➡ Butterfly Blenny

Lives on shelly or rocky bottoms in depths of 10–100m. It often "owns" a broken pot or hollow in which it lays its eggs in spring. 20cm

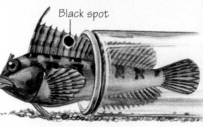

Black spot

Male guarding nest in jar

Wrinkled, grey skin

⬆ Wolf-fish

On rocky bottoms 20–300m deep. Eats sea urchins, crabs and whelks. Crushes shells with its big, peg-like teeth. North Atlantic only. 1.2m

⬇ Dragonet

Near the bottom, 20–100m deep. Often buries itself. Eats molluscs, crustaceans and worms. 20cm

Breeding male displaying long fins

Wavy stripes

Round shape

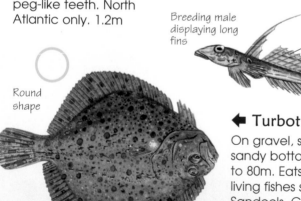

⬅ Turbot

On gravel, shelly and sandy bottoms down to 80m. Eats bottom-living fishes such as Sandeels, Gobies and Dragonets. 80cm

➡ Wide-eyed Flounder

Shallow sandy areas.
Feeds on small fishes
and crustaceans. Male's
eyes spaced wide apart.
Mediterranean. 20cm

Eyes

Male

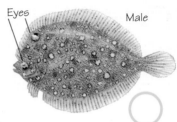

Rounded
tail

Orange
spots

⬅ Plaice

Common seabed
fish on sandy, muddy
and gravel bottoms.
Feeds mainly on
shellfish, worms and
crustaceans. 50cm

➡ Halibut

Largest flatfish.
Depth of 100–1500m
on mud, sand and
gravel. Hunts for
fishes in midwater.
North Atlantic. 2m

Diamond
shape

Big mouth

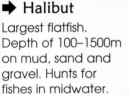

Square
tail

All these fishes
can camouflage
themselves by
changing colour

➡ Sole

Common flatfish. Burrows
in sandy bottom. Comes
out to hunt worms and
crustaceans at night.
Young in sandy pools
on the beach. 40cm

Black tip
on fin

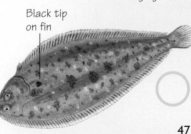

Coastal midwater fishes

Most midwater fishes in coastal waters (up to 100m deep) live in schools. Only the largest fishes can survive without a school's protection.

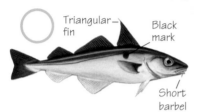

Triangular fin
Black mark
Short barbel

← Haddock

Lives close to seabed in depths of 40–300m. Eats bottom-living brittlestars, worms, molluscs and fishe North Atlantic. 75cm

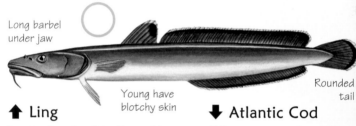

Long barbel under jaw

Young have blotchy skin

Rounded tail

↑ Ling

Long, slender fish. Found by rocks and wrecks as deep as 400m. Eats mainly fishes and crustaceans. Rare in the Mediterranean. 2m

↓ Atlantic Cod

Often near seabed. Big schools in midwater. Eats a wide variety of fishes and crustaceans. Northe Europe only. Overfished. 1.2m

Snout juts over lower jaw

↓ Hake

Lives in quite deep water, just above the bottom, coming nearer the surface at night. Eats fishes and squid, and, when young, crustaceans. 1.8m

Adults have white lateral line

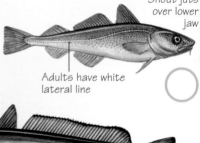

No barbel

Square-cut tail

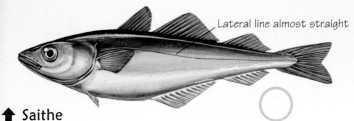

Lateral line almost straight

↑ Saithe

Also called Coalfish or Coley. Young fish live near the shore, larger ones in big schools in open water. Eats fishes and crustaceans. Northern Europe only. 1.3m

↓ Pouting

Very large schools on sandy bottoms when young; close to rocks and reefs when adults. Eats shrimp and small fishes. 41cm

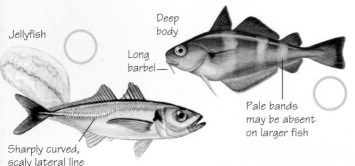

Jellyfish

Deep body

Long barbel

Pale bands may be absent on larger fish

Sharply curved, scaly lateral line

↑ Horse Mackerel

In great numbers near the shore and far out to sea. Young fishes swim in groups under jellyfishes. 30cm

↓ Greater Amberjack

In small schools near rocky outcrops and islands. Migrates long distances. Young float under jellyfishes. Rare in north Atlantic. 1m

Deeply forked tail

Amber stripe

49

Coastal midwater fishes

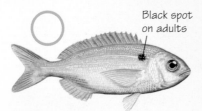

Black spot on adults

← Red Sea-bream

In schools when young, but adults form only small groups and live in deeper water (to 100m). Eats fishes, crustaceans and squid. 50cm

→ Black Sea-bream

Lives around wrecks and rocky outcrops close to sand. Hollows a nest in the sand for the eggs, which the male guards until they hatch. 35cm

Breeding males turn black

← Saupe

Swims in dense schools in shallow water. Grazes fine algae off rocks and seaweeds. Not in northern Europe. 30cm

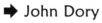

Yellow stripes

→ Spiny Dogfish

These little sharks form huge, single-sex schools and hunt Herring, Sprats and Sandeels. At depths of 10–90m, nearer the surface at night. 1.1m

Spines

→ John Dory

Swims slowly. Lives alone. Waits in the shadows for small fishes and snaps them up in its huge, extending jaws. 40cm

Coastal open ocean fishes

Open ocean fishes are mostly plankton-eaters, such as Mackerel, or fishes that hunt them, such as Porbeagle sharks. Smaller fishes live in schools and most are silvery or white underneath and blue-green above.

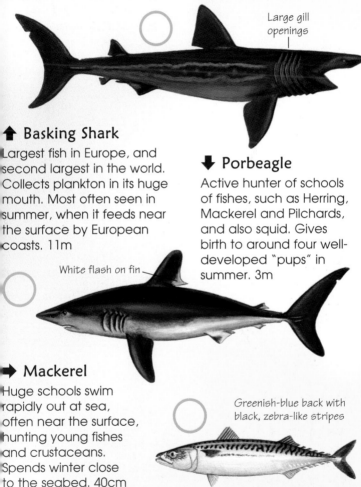

Large gill openings

⬆ Basking Shark

Largest fish in Europe, and second largest in the world. Collects plankton in its huge mouth. Most often seen in summer, when it feeds near the surface by European coasts. 11m

White flash on fin

⬇ Porbeagle

Active hunter of schools of fishes, such as Herring, Mackerel and Pilchards, and also squid. Gives birth to around four well-developed "pups" in summer. 3m

➡ Mackerel

Huge schools swim rapidly out at sea, often near the surface, hunting young fishes and crustaceans. Spends winter close to the seabed. 40cm

Greenish-blue back with black, zebra-like stripes

Coastal open ocean fishes

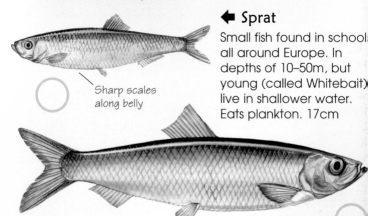

← Sprat

Small fish found in schools all around Europe. In depths of 10–50m, but young (called Whitebait) live in shallower water. Eats plankton. 17cm

Sharp scales along belly

↑ Herring

Huge schools near the surface. Migrates along coasts. Eats young fishes and small crustaceans. Eaten by larger fishes, seabirds and dolphins. Not in Mediterranean. 43cm

↓ Pilchard

Common in schools from Britain southwards. Eats small crustaceans and other plankton. Lays eggs in spring and summer. Young are called Sardines. 25cm

Ridges on gill cover

Large scales

→ Anchovy

Lives in vast schools. Found as far north as the Dutch coast. Eats plankton, especially crustacean and fish larvae. 20cm

Short lower jaw

Young fish: upper jaw shorter than lower

⬆ Garpike

Fast-swimming fish, common at the surface where it hunts young fishes, such as Herring and Sandeels. Their eggs have long threads which tangle with floating seaweeds. Tasty to eat, but people are often put off by its green bones. 94cm

Fins set far back on body

⬇ Barracuda

Common in Mediterranean, and Atlantic south of Spain. Younger fish live in large schools, usually near the surface. They attack small fishes with swift, snapping bites. Larger Barracudas tend to live alone. 60cm

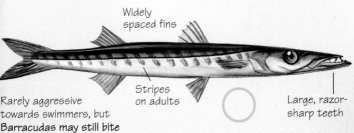

Widely spaced fins

Stripes on adults

Rarely aggressive towards swimmers, but Barracudas may still bite

Large, razor-sharp teeth

⬇ Smooth Hammerhead

Solitary* shark. Often found by rocky reefs at less than 20m depth. Its widely spaced nostrils help it to sniff out the direction of fishes, crustaceans and squid to eat. Southern Europe. 4m

The only type of Hammerhead found in Europe

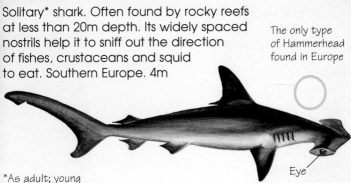

*As adult; young may form schools

Eye

Offshore open ocean fishes

Most surface-living ocean fishes are blue-green above, white or silvery below. Many hunt smaller, plankton-eating fishes that live in schools. These ocean hunters spend their lives on the move, travelling thousands of miles a year.

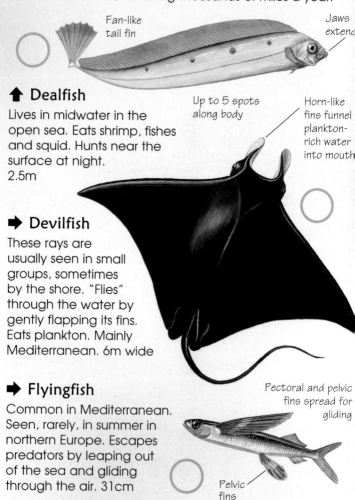

Fan-like tail fin

Jaws extend

↑ Dealfish

Lives in midwater in the open sea. Eats shrimp, fishes and squid. Hunts near the surface at night.
2.5m

Up to 5 spots along body

Horn-like fins funnel plankton-rich water into mouth

→ Devilfish

These rays are usually seen in small groups, sometimes by the shore. "Flies" through the water by gently flapping its fins. Eats plankton. Mainly Mediterranean. 6m wide

→ Flyingfish

Common in Mediterranean. Seen, rarely, in summer in northern Europe. Escapes predators by leaping out of the sea and gliding through the air. 31cm

Pectoral and pelvic fins spread for gliding

Pelvic fins

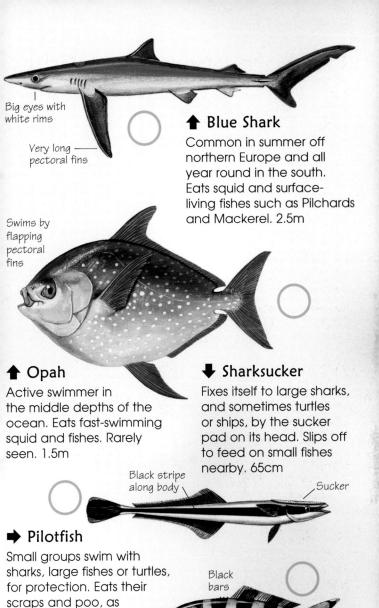

Big eyes with white rims

Very long pectoral fins

Swims by flapping pectoral fins

↑ Blue Shark

Common in summer off northern Europe and all year round in the south. Eats squid and surface-living fishes such as Pilchards and Mackerel. 2.5m

↑ Opah

Active swimmer in the middle depths of the ocean. Eats fast-swimming squid and fishes. Rarely seen. 1.5m

↓ Sharksucker

Fixes itself to large sharks, and sometimes turtles or ships, by the sucker pad on its head. Slips off to feed on small fishes nearby. 65cm

Black stripe along body

Sucker

➡ Pilotfish

Small groups swim with sharks, large fishes or turtles, for protection. Eats their scraps and poo, as well as small fishes and crustaceans. 40cm

Black bars

55

Offshore open ocean fishes

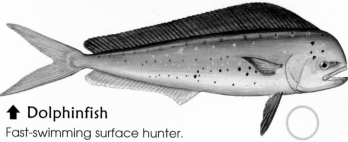

↑ Dolphinfish

Fast-swimming surface hunter.
Skin changes colour. May flash
with neon blue patterns when
caught. Forehead steepens
with age. 1.9m

← Bluefish

Ferocious predator.
Forms schools and
attacks smaller fishes.
In a feeding frenzy,
it will even chase
them onto a beach.
Mediterranean, south
Atlantic. 60cm

➡ Atlantic Pomfret

A midwater fish that
migrates northwards
and is often stranded
on northern coasts.
Feeds on small fishes,
crustaceans and
squid. 55cm

Flattened rugby-
ball shape

← Scabbardfish

Found in water 100-
400m deep over
sandy and muddy
bottoms. Eats mainly
fishes. Caught by
deep-sea fishermen
and trawlers. 2m

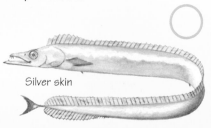

Silver skin

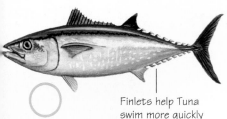

← Bluefin Tuna

Large, superb swimmer. In warm seas, visiting northern Europe in summer. Eats crustaceans and fishes. Endangered by overfishing. 4m

Finlets help Tuna swim more quickly

→ Albacore Tuna

In warm seas. Rare visitor to UK. Eats all kinds of fishes, squid and shrimp. Its meat is much paler than that of other Tunas. Overfished. 1.3m

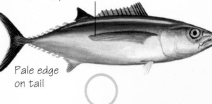

Very long pectoral fins

Pale edge on tail

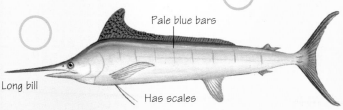

Pale blue bars

Long bill

Has scales

↑ White Marlin

Rare surface-living fish which migrates along the warm mid-Atlantic coasts. Feeds on fishes. Acrobatic, leaping above the water. 2.5m

↓ Swordfish

Lives from the surface down to 600m. Hunts schools of fishes such as Mackerel and Pilchards. Defends itself from sharks by slashing with its bill. Rare. 4.9m

The fastest fishes have crescent-shaped tail fins

Very long, sharp bill

Adults have no scales

No pelvic fins

57

Offshore open ocean fishes

➡ Ocean Sunfish

Heaviest bony fish. Feeds mainly
on Moon Jellyfishes. Lives near
the surface of the sea, where
it may be seen lying on its side.
This looks like sunbathing,
giving rise to its name.
4m (dorsal to anal
fin tips)

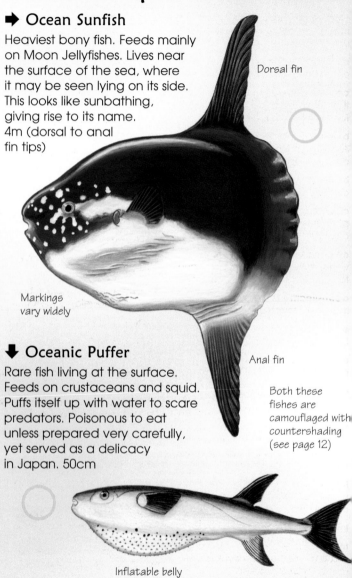

Dorsal fin

Markings
vary widely

⬇ Oceanic Puffer

Rare fish living at the surface.
Feeds on crustaceans and squid.
Puffs itself up with water to scare
predators. Poisonous to eat
unless prepared very carefully,
yet served as a delicacy
in Japan. 50cm

Anal fin

Both these
fishes are
camouflaged with
countershading
(see page 12)

Inflatable belly

Useful words

algae – a group of simple, plant-like living things ranging from green slime to giant seaweed

barbels – chin feelers, used to probe for food on the bottom

barnacle – a type of *crustacean* that lives stuck to a rock, catching food scraps with feathery limbs

breeding – mating and laying eggs. At breeding time, male fish often display breeding colours.

brittlestar – a skinny, starfish-like creature

camouflage – a body colour, pattern or shape that helps an animal to hide from view

crustaceans – a group of creatures with several pairs of jointed legs and tough outer shells, such as crabs

downstream – in the direction a river flows, towards the sea

endangered – in danger of becoming *extinct*

estuary – a place where a river meets the sea

extinct – died out completely

fry – newly hatched fish

larva – (plural: **larvae**) the young stage of an egg-born creature such as a fish or *crustacean*, which looks different from the adult

lateral line – an organ that senses vibrations in the water. It shows as a line running along a fish's side.

lowland – a low-lying region

migrate – regularly move from one place to another, and back again, usually to feed or *breed*

molluscs – a group of soft-bodied creatures, often with protective shells, such as limpets and snails

overfishing – catching so many fish that their population is threatened

oxygenated – containing the gas oxygen, which is vital for life

parasite – a living thing that lives on or in another one, causing it harm

plankton – tiny sea animals and plants that drift with the currents, such as *crustacean larvae*

predator – an animal that hunts and eats other animals

prey – an animal that is hunted and eaten by other animals

school – a group of fish that live and swim together

sea cucumber – a simple, tube-shaped animal related to starfish

spiracle – a breathing hole

stagnant – still and poorly *oxygenated*

sucker fin – a sucker-like fin used by some fishes to cling to rocks

tentacle – an elongated growth, for example on a fish's head

territory – an area an animal defends as its own

upland – an area of high ground

upstream – against the direction a river flows, towards its source

venomous – containing venom, a substance that causes pain or medical problems if it enters the body through the skin (whereas poison enters through the mouth)

Scorecard

When you start spotting, you'll soon find that some fishes are rarer than others. To give you a rough idea of how likely you are to see them, all the fishes in the book are listed here with a score next to each one. Common species score 5 points; those that are rarest or hardest to spot are worth 25. If you like, you can use the "Spotted" boxes to record when or where you saw each species.

Species	Score	Spotted	Species	Score	Spotted
Albacore Tuna	15		Bream	5	
Anchovy	10		Bullhead	10	
Angelshark	25		Burbot	25	
Anglerfish	15		Butterfish	5	
Arctic Charr	15		Butterfly Blenny	15	
Asp	25		Cardinalfish	20	
Atlantic Cod	5		Chub	5	
Atlantic Pomfret	20		Comber	20	
Ballan Wrasse	5		Common Carp	5	
Barbel	10		Conger Eel	10	
Barracuda	20		Crucian Carp	5	
Basking Shark	15		Cuckoo Wrasse	10	
Bitterling	20		Dab	5	
Black-faced Blenny	20		Dace	5	
Black Sea-bream	10		Damselfish	15	
Bleak	10		Dealfish	25	
Bluefin Tuna	20		Devilfish	25	
Bluefish	20		Dolphinfish	20	
Blue Shark	20		Dragonet	5	

Eckström's Topknot	20		Mediterranean Toothcarp	20	
Eelpout	10		Minnow	5	
Electric Ray	20		Montagu's Blenny	15	
European Eel	10		Moray Eel	20	
Fivebeard Rockling	5		Mudminnow	25	
Five-spotted Wrasse	20		Nase	25	
Flounder	5		Ninespine Stickleback	10	
Flyingfish	15		Oceanic Puffer	25	
Flying Gurnard	20		Ocean Sunfish	20	
Garpike	10		Ocellated Wrasse	20	
Goldfish	5		Opah	25	
Goldsinny Wrasse	10		Ornate Wrasse	10	
Grayling	15		Parrotfish	20	
Greater Amberjack	20		Peacock Blenny	20	
Greater Pipefish	10		Pearlfish	25	
Grey Triggerfish	15		Perch	5	
Gudgeon	5		Pike	5	
Haddock	5		Pilchard	10	
Hake	10		Pilotfish	25	
Halibut	10		Plaice	5	
Herring	5		Pollack	5	
Hooknose	15		Porbeagle	20	
Horse Mackerel	5		Pouting	5	
John Dory	10		Powan	20	
Lampern	10		Rainbow Trout	5	
Lesser Weever	10		Rainbow Wrasse	10	
Ling	10		Red Bandfish	20	
Lumpsucker	10		Red Mullet	15	
Mackerel	5		Red Sea-bream	15	
Meagre	20		Roach	5	

Rock Goby	5		Stargazer	20
Rudd	10		Stingray	20
Ruffe	15		Stone Loach	5
Saddled Bream	15		Streber	20
Saithe	5		Sturgeon	25
Salmon	10		Swordfish	25
Sand Goby	5		Tench	10
Sand Smelt	10		Thicklip Grey Mullet	5
Sand Tiger	15		Thinlip Grey Mullet	10
Saupe	20		Thornback Ray	5
Sawfish	25		Three-spined Stickleback	5
Scabbardfish	25		Trout	5
Scorpionfish	20		Tub Gurnard	15
Seabass	15		Turbot	5
Sea Lamprey	15		Twaite Shad	25
Sea Scorpion	5		Two-banded Bream	15
Sea Stickleback	15		Two-spotted Goby	10
Shanny	5		Vendace	20
Sharksucker	20		Weatherfish	20
Shore Clingfish	10		Wels Catfish	25
Shore Rockling	5		White Marlin	25
Short-snouted Seahorse	20		Whiting	5
Silver Bream	10		Wide-eyed Flounder	15
Small Sandeel	5		Wolf-fish	15
Small-spotted Catshark	10		Worm Pipefish	5
Smooth Hammerhead	25		Zander	10
Sole	5		Ziege	25
Spined Loach	15			
Spiny Dogfish	15			
Sprat	5			

Index

Designed by Reuben Barrance. Digital manipulation by Keith Furnival.
With thanks to Victoria Richards.

Additional illustrations by Christine Howes, Joyce Bee and Ian Jackson

PHOTO CREDITS: Cover (Saupe) Anestis Rekkas/Alamy (weed) Prof. Dr. Albert Kok;
1 (Perch) © blickwinkel/Alamy; 2–3 (Barracudas) Wild Wonders of Europe/Pitkin/
naturepl.com; 10–11 © Horizon International Images Limited/Alamy

This edition first published in 2010 by Usborne Publishing Ltd.
Usborne House, 83–85 Saffron Hill, London, EC1N 8RT, England.
Copyright © 2010, 1978 Usborne Publishing Ltd. The name Usborne
and the devices ♕ ♛ are Trade Marks of Usborne Publishing Ltd.

Printed in Shenzhen, Guangdong, China